Scattered Thoughts Vol II

More Words from Him to Me and You

(The Devotional)

Scattered Thoughts Vol II

More Words from Him to Me and You

(The Devotional)

Oregean Adams

Copyright©2019 Oregean Adams. All rights reserved.

No part of this book may be reproduced in any written, electronic, recording, or photocopying without written permission of the publisher or author. The exception would be in the case of brief quotations embodied in the critical articles or reviews and pages where permission is specifically granted by the publisher or author.

Holy Bible Scriptures found in NIV, KJV, NKJV, and CEV.

Books may be purchased by contacting the publisher or the author.

Cover Design: Ministering Moments

Publisher:
Butterfly Typeface Publishing,
Little Rock Arkansas

Editor: Iris. M. Williams

ISBN 978-1-947656-53-6

1. Religion

2. Inspirational

3. Spirituality

First Edition

Printed in the United States

Dedication

Inspired by the Holy Ghost, written for you!

"Now to Him who is able to do exceedingly abundantly above all that we ask or think, according to the power that works in us, to Him be glory in the church by Christ Jesus to all generations, forever and ever. Amen."

Ephesians 3:20-21 NKJV

Table of Contents

Preface 17

Beautifully Single 19

God Cannot Lie 23

What Is So Great About Being Great? 25

Deliverance From Sins 27

You Are Blessed When You Give 29

The Lord's Will Be Done 31

The Invitation Has Gone Out 33

Charge The Debt To Me 35

The Clouds How Awesome They Are 37

An Unchangeable Savior 39

The Power Is In Your Tongue 41

Disciple or Deserter 43

Forgetting God 45

Following But Not Really Understanding 47

Do Not Remember 49

Inspired By My Brother In Christ 51

Spirit And Life 53

Day And Night Word 55

Become What His Word Say's 57

Where Is Your Treasure? 59

The Little Man 61

Sowing Seed And Reaping A Harvest....................65

I Believe God....................69

Godly Goals....................71

Watch Out For Those Snakes In Your Life....................73

The Attributes Of God....................75

Moving By The Power Of God....................77

My Birth Date....................79

Will You Be Ready When Jesus Comes?....................81

Please Answer Me Oh Lord....................83

From Revelation To Reality....................85

God's Oracles....................87

He Said It....................89

If You Want To See God Look Up....................91

Working, But Not Out Of Love....................93

Abraham Father Of Faith....................97

Does What You Are Doing Line Up?....................99

An Unusual Request....................101

Master Publisher....................103

Our Gracious God....................105

Because Of His Mercy....................109

Forever God....................111

The Glory Of The Lord....................113

The Requirements Of The Lord....................115

Satan The Tempter....................117

God's Victory..119

Baptism..123

Keep On Going..127

His Merciful Kindness..129

About the Author..131

Also by Oregean Adams

Scattered Thoughts (Volume I)

Foreword

My relationship with Christ is something that I've never taken lightly. I've always attended church service, been an active member in ministry, and made sure that I wasn't just walking around carrying the title "Christian." It is my consistent goal to become closer to Christ. You know... a truly intimate relationship. A relationship that not only involves him knowing all about me and having a daily yearning to spend time with me, but one where I share the exact same feelings. However, this has not only been a goal of mine, but also a struggle.

Throughout my adult life, I've unintentionally found myself often letting life and all that comes along with it get in the way of developing that genuine rock-solid relationship with Christ. After having the opportunity to read *Scattered Thoughts*, I have been impacted tremendously! Not only has it pushed me to want to learn and grow more in my studies of God's Word, but it's made it a lot easier! I was so frustrated with books and articles I'd tried reading in the past that never help and often only confused me even more. Oregean Adams, however, writes and discusses topics in a way that anyone could follow!

I truly believe that she is God ordained and destined to be a blessing to the people of God by sharing her wisdom and knowledge of his word, not only through what she has read and been taught but definitely based on her experiences. I'm blessed to know her first as my mother, secondly as my friend, and now as a great author! I trust that her writings will be a blessing to each and everyone that picks it up and reads it.

Congratulations and Many Blessings to you Mommy!

Love Always,

Chelsea B. Adams, M.S.

Acknowledgments

I also want to thank my Family for the Love that we share beginning with my husband Mitchell B. Adams; words cannot express how much I appreciate you.

To my children Helen L. Leniear, Pamela D. Ferrell, Kerry L. Ferrell, and Chelsea B. Adams; I love you dearly... I share this book with you. It is a great honor to be called Mama by you. It is also a great honor to have been chosen by Almighty God (EL SHADDAI) to do this great work.

I pray and thank God for all of you daily, along with my beautiful grandchildren: and for all of my other family members who are too numerous to name. God bless,

To Be Continued...

Preface

"And the Lord said to me; your Latter shall be greater
(Haggai 2:9)."

This Book is dedicated to my beloved Pastor, Eric L. Alexander for his awesome teaching and preaching ability, and for his boldness in speaking the gospel of Our Lord and Savior, "Jesus Christ."

A part of the name of this book is also through the inspiration of my Pastor.

This Book has been created to help you in your daily walk with God. Step into its pages and let it take hold of you. You can read it daily, or you can read it all at once. But let the Holy Spirit guide you as you read, and go through the Scriptures, believe me, *He* is here.

Beautifully Single

(1 Corinthians 6:13b.)

Male and Female

It does not make any difference who you are. If you are single and a Christian, you have a great responsibility to the Lord.

There is a certain way that you are to live, and there is a certain way that you are to carry yourself in this world.

If you are going to please the Lord; then you need to follow the Logos Word (written).

Everything that your body desires to do is not to be carried out.

If you are obedient to the Lord, then the Logos Word will become the Ramah Word, (it will live inside of you).

Submission is not just for those who are married; it is for every Christian.

You are not to put yourself in a position where you will fall to the temptation of your sexual desires.

You know what those temptations are, and you know whom!

So, you need to stay far from them; you do not want to be tempted beyond what you are able to control, you know exactly what makes you weak.

Stop sitting around and thinking about ways that you can get him or her to come to you and stop listening to that music that works your mind and body...you know what it is.

You are to put on the armor of God, and you will be able to stand through your temptation!

Pick up the Bible and read it every day; find those scriptures that pertain to what you are going through.

Prayerfully choose you a Christian friend, sister or brother; that will help you to be accountable for your actions, one who will not baby you, someone that will not cater to your whims but will boldly let you know that you need to step back in line.

When you do this, it pleases the Lord; He knows that you are trying, and therefore will bless you.

Jesus can and will use you; your body and your spirit belong to Him (1 Corinthians 6:17).

After all, there's too much work to be done before the coming of the New Kingdom.

There are lives that need to be saved. It is my prayer that you see how important it is to keep your mind and your body pure before the Lord and for the Lord.

A SCATTERED THOUGHT TO PONDER:

Your few minutes of pleasure could result in the loss of a soul; ask yourself is it really worth it?

God Cannot Lie

(Titus 1:2)

God of Truth!

God has given us a promise in His Word that will last forever and ever.

It is the promise of eternal life in Jesus Christ.

For those who have doubts about it, you can be assured today.

Eternal life is real, and you shall have it but only if you have given your life back to the Father through His Son Jesus Christ.

There are no tricks, and there are no gimmicks; God said it, and that's it.

God never goes back on His Word; before this would take place, heaven and earth would definitely pass away.

From where I sit, and by what I can see, we are still here; it is because His Word is Truth.

There are people who would choose to go against what the Father has promised.

There is nothing that you or I can do about that, except to pray; that they would come to their senses before it is everlasting too late.

I am glad that He loved us enough to make a way for us.

I am glad that He has given us the One, through who we can have eternal life.

I am glad that He is Jesus Christ, the Son of the Living God.

Jesus has died for us once. It will never happen again; now you have a choice, and it is solely up to you, as to whether or not you will receive His wonderful gift and live forever more.

He has focused Himself totally on us so why not do the same and focus yourself totally on Him.

You have a great opportunity right now; it is to give thanks to the Lord, for His loving you as He does.

There will never be another who will love you as Jesus does.

Not in this world, nor in the one to come, nobody will ever love you as the Lord loves you.

A Scattered thought to ponder:

You have been made an heir to His throne, it is a precious gift that will never wear out; or rust out, just how long is forever?

What Is So Great About Being Great?

(Matthew 23:11)

Why Is It So Important?

What is it about being popular that makes people go to great lengths to achieve it?

Isn't it something that you can teach what you are not living? What does that make you? If you teach, teach with the love of God, and for no other reason.

According to the Word and the warnings of Jesus, this makes you a hypocrite.

If the work that you are doing; and you do it to be seen, then you are a hypocrite.

If it is not about the Lord, but it is about, "wow look at me," then you are a hypocrite.

If what you are doing is not lifting up the name of Jesus, then your work is in vain.

You may be the best teacher in the world, you may be a good speaker, and you may be good at getting things done, but, if you are doing it because you know that you will get an honorable mention, you are a hypocrite.

If all you want to do is be out front; and never work behind the scenes, doing the kind of things that do not often get mentioned, oh yes, again; you are a hypocrite.

People who love the Lord, and do His will from their heart, do not care if they get mentioned or not.

Being a show off does not in any way impress God; God looks at the heart of a man. You should not go after a title just for the sake of having one.

He speaks about us having brotherly love for one another, so I definitely should not flaunt what God has given unto me; it is a gift to be used to His satisfaction, not mine. Whatever you do; then do it according to the will of God, not out of pride and what somebody else may say about you, because it won't last.

Serving the Master – Teacher is more important than anything you could ever do; it is more important than any place of honor, that the world could ever offer you, so be the servant that He has called you to be, and then you will be pleasing in His sight.

A Scattered thought to ponder:

Why is it that you want people to live their lives a certain way, and you are not doing it yourself?

Deliverance From Sins

(Romans 6:14)

Penalty and Power

God has fixed it so that sin will not be our master.

He has given man a way out of the negative things that he finds himself involved in. Our way out is "The Lord Jesus Christ."

If you are still living a sinful life, it is certainly not because you have to; it is because you choose to.

Jesus Christ came down to earth, lived as an example for us, suffered for us, then bled and died for all of our sins.

We are now living in a time where you know without any doubt, that you do not have to remain lost.

The Holy Ghost has gained more freedom to operate in the lives of the saved now than He has had in decades; most Christians have become very open and obedient to His leading because they are now in tune to the teaching of His Word.

We have been released under the power of the Holy Ghost to live God-fearing lives.

We are not to live the way that people lived in the days of Lot; and His wife, when there was much sin among the people.

The truth be told, you cannot tell that much of a difference in some people today, because they are doing some of everything; and living all kind of ways, they have no respect for anything, or anybody.

Christian people are still lying and cheating one another and being disobedient to the Word of God. His Word informs us that we do not have to live Christ-less lives.

The Holy Scriptures are saying: children of God; you are no longer under the law, but you are now under Grace. Grace is; God's unmerited favor, Grace is a gift that God has given us.

We have done nothing to deserve it; but because of His love for us, we have it. If you were still under the law, It would be your master.

Just imagine trying to live all those laws that were written by Moses in the Old Testament. It would be utterly impossible for you to move even one inch because sin would rule over you, and you would already be on your way to hell.

You have Grace, but you are not doing anything to make a difference in your life. His grace really is, and without a doubt sufficient for you, try it, you will love it.

A Scattered thought to ponder:

How will you ever be able to move forward if you never say yes to God's gracious gift, that gift that will last throughout eternity?

You Are Blessed When You Give

(Acts 20:35)

So Why Don't You?

There are people who have been blessed beyond belief, who have the means to help turn this world around.

But they refuse to do so; there are people who feel that they are not obligated to anyone but themselves, they sit and watch people suffer, but they will not reach out to them, this makes for a sad situation.

God has not blessed you dears, just for the sake of you having; He has blessed you that you would in return bless others.

The more you give, the more He will give to you, it will not always be money, but I assure you, you will be blessed indeed.

The rich man thought in his heart that all he possessed was his, but; he found out later that God was not pleased with him at all.

The decision that God made about him was a final one, God said, thy fool, your soul is required of you tonight.

So, don't think that He does not see what you are doing, and what is going on with you, and around you. He knows it all.

I know that there are people who have money, but they will not share it in any way. If you are a born-again believer, then it becomes your obligation to help.

There are many ministries that you can give to, and there are people working to help the people of the world, but they don't have what it takes to get the job done.

There are people in need all over our nation, and the world. Why don't you say a prayer about being loosed to reach out with your wealth?

Let God show you where He wants you to begin sowing and planting your seeds.

One of the best places that a Christian can sow, if you have not already begun; is in the house of God. If you have a church home give to her, after all, charity does begin at home. Please be assured that it is truly more blessed to give than to receive.

I will close this lesson with a little nugget called a Coin phrase: When what I do pleases God, then I know that what I do is a good thing.

A Scattered thought to ponder:

What about you are you pleasing your Father; or are you just pleasing yourself? Remember, the Lord is watching; so, let your decision be the right one in His sight.

The Lord's Will Be Done

(Acts 21:14)

That Is What Counts.

Have you ever given thought to the fact that you are saved, but still want to run your own life? Yes, it is true; there are a lot of saved people, who just will not let the Holy Ghost have rule in their lives. You are hurting yourself.

There's a process that we go through, even though we are saved.

One step is to give up your rights to you; because being born again, you are no longer your own, you no longer belong to you.

This is something that we all must and should do; because God does not want part of you, He wants all of you.

How can He use you, if you will not yield yourself to Him? He has put wonderful and awesome gifts inside of you, but they cannot be fully used until you give yourself totally over to His will.

This seems to be a no, no, for some Christians; it is either their way or no way at all.

There are a few, who choose to yield their will to God, here and there, and it is only on a Sunday morning, and some of those, are not even a full two hours. Do you think that you are doing Him some sort of favor?

If you do, please be assured, this is not giving of yourself totally; this is ritual, and this is a habit, it can also be defined as a tradition for some.

Being a true follower of God comes with an inner will, a will that says I have to let go of the things that I want and grab hold of what God has for me.

If you yield your will to the Lord things are going to change tremendously for you.

I look at our young children, and I can see how good it would be for them; if they could only see the blessing that He has in store for them. Especially while they have that youthful strength, and while their memory is at its highest peak.

Oh, how God could use you, but, the ball is in your court; God will not force you to do anything for Him. But what an honor, and what a privilege it would be what an honor to have an opportunity to serve the Lord. When you commit to Him, what seems hard becomes easy. So trust Him now, to see you to it, because what He sees you to, He will definitely see you through.

A SCATTERED THOUGHT TO PONDER:

Why not let His will be done inside of you?

The Invitation Has Gone Out

(Isaiah 9: St. Luke 2:1-11)

Did You Get Yours?

There is a celebration going on, and you have been invited!

If you did not get an invitation, it's because you have refused Him.

The invitation went out over two thousand years ago, and it went something like this:

> **UNTO US, A CHILD IS GIVEN.**
>
> **UNTO US A SAVIOR IS HE.**
>
> **HIS NAME IS JESUS CHRIST THE LORD.**
>
> **HE IS THE SON OF GOD.**
>
> **HE WAS BORN IN A MANAGER IN BETHLEHEM AMONG THE CATTLE.**
>
> **SUCH A PLACE WOULD HAVE BEEN UNACCEPTABLE FOR YOU AND ME.**
>
> **WON'T YOU COME AND SEE THE PLACE WHERE HE LAY?**
>
> **HE WAS BORN OF A VIRGIN; WHOSE NAME WAS MARY.**
>
> **SHE WAS CHOSEN BY GOD AND CONFIRMED BY THE ANGEL GABRIEL.**

She was engaged to a man named Joseph, who came to understand the nature of her pregnancy, because of this same angel.

His birth was not a mistake; it was intentional, it happened for the sake of all mankind.

The invitation farther reads:

He did not complain; He did what He had to do in order to save mankind from eternal damnation, (second death).

He didn't stop there.

He went from birth to the cross at Calvary.

He died for you and me; He was crucified with two thieves, one on His right, and one on His left.

You may not have been there physically that day in the flesh, but there you truly were.

When He gave up the ghost and went back to His Father in heaven, He freed us from all of our sins.

He opened a door that can never be shut; but it can be missed if you don't surrender your life back to Him, trust Him, He's Worthy. This is the door that will lead you to everlasting life in Jesus Christ, who is Lord and Savior. Hallelujah, Amen.

A SCATTERED THOUGHT TO PONDER:

Don't you find this invitation worthy of accepting?

Charge the Debt To Me

(Philemon1: 18)

Love For A Brother Or A Sister

Though Paul did not name what Onesimus might have done, it could have; and possibly involved money. Money makes the best of us a little bit crazy, but you should not let it rule you.

Onesimus was a salve, so this could have been a reason to take something that did not belong to him.

Slaves did not have the best, and they were not treated the best, in most cases, they had to do what the Master told them to do.

It was not a matter of whether they wanted to do; what they were told to do, they had to.

There is a real possibility that he stole whatever he needed in order to survive. This may have caused a loss for his master Philemon.

Paul did not judge him; he simply stated, "If he owes you anything, charge it to me."

How awesome, that he would put himself in the place of his brother, that is unconditional love. What would you have done in this situation?

I can hear you now. There is an old saying that I grew up with: you made your bed, now you have to lay in it. I am sure you can think of one or two of these type sayings as well.

In that day, the word 'charge' was an accounting term, meaning he [Paul] would pay. Can you see how Paul is standing in the gap for his friend?

It reminds me of Jesus Christ, and how He went on that cross at Calvary for all mankind. That was the greatest debt ever to be paid; and, Jesus Christ was the only one who could pay that enormous bill.

Every time someone comes to Christ, his or her debt has already been paid. The same way that Onesimus was indebted to Paul, so are we to Jesus Christ.

Paul had nothing to do with the guilt part of this debt, yet he stood up for him. Jesus Christ has done the same for us. Now, won't you be a blessing, by standing up for someone else? By doing so, you help to bridge the gap between that individual and the Lord Jesus Christ.

It's wonderful, to be involved, especially when someone brings his or her soul back home to the Lord.

A Scattered thought to ponder:

Can you recall a time in your life when you took something that did not belong to you? You took it simply because you wanted it.

The Clouds How Awesome They Are

(Nahum 1:3b.)

God's Feet

I have read the Bible over and over, many times not to be a show-off, but to learn more about my Father.

In my reading experience last year, I read up on this particular Scripture.

I want to share it with as many as I possibly can.

It gave me a new outlook on how I view His creation.

When I read this Scripture, I could not get passed it; I kept coming back, just looking in amazement at what it is saying about the Father.

When I read the Word of God, I prepare myself for His Word to get up off of the pages, because that is what it does for me.

It lives, it does not remain Logos (written Word); it becomes Ramah (living Word).

I know that we all look up from time to time, and I know that we see, or have seen things or formations in the clouds, but never would I have ever imagined such a thing as the clouds being the dust of His feet, now I really look at them, and they are beautiful, but they have taken on a new meaning in me!

There are days when they are just sitting there, and I say to myself, "The Father is not moving a lot today."

Then there are days when I look at them, and they are moving fast like they are on their way somewhere else.

I say within my inner man; my, my, God is really getting things done today, He is moving by His holy power.

I don't know what this is going to leave you thinking, but to put it in perspective; He is so great, that the clouds are like dust under His feet.

It makes me very happy to know that God is even in control over the inanimate things. He is controlling nature, He is controlling evil, and He could be controlling whatever is troubling you right now.

Nothing gets past the Father; we should all be so grateful that it does not.

I praise Him for what He is doing in your life, and in mine, I praise Him for what He is going to do, and I praise Him for what He has already done because He is oh so worthy of our praise.

A Scattered thought to ponder:

What has God done in your life that is worthy of praise?

An Unchangeable Savior

(Hebrews 13:8)

Jesus Christ

I don't understand how man can deny the One, who died for them; who gave His life for them.

It is a puzzling thing for me, yet it is as real as we are living, and breathing.

What I find to be so devastating is that God has given us all a mind that knows that Jesus is real and that He is who He claims to be, and that is The Lord and Savior of this world.

Yet there are people perishing each and every day without Him; they are dying out of Christ because they refuse to believe.

We who have been born again have a great work to do; the Lord depends on us to get the job done.

We have to be bold disciples, it's not good enough to watch those that are lost go from day to day, and not do anything to try and reach them.

Each one of us has someone that we need to reach.

There are people all around you who need to know about Jesus, and receive Him into their hearts, and be saved.

Some go to work day in, and day out; but what are you doing with what you have learned?

Have you ever had the opportunity to witness to someone, but did not?

Have you ever came back looking for the person, and found out that the person you could have been a witness to had died?

Well, this is where it stands now with those that do not know the Lord.

If you would see them as they really are, I believe that it would move you. Remember, you were there once too.

Unsaved people really are dead, until you reach out to them; so don't let another moment pass without being a witness to someone who crosses your path.

I am sure it is not an easy thing to do, especially if you have not been trained on how to witness properly. Let the Holy Ghost lead you, for He will; and He certainly knows what He is doing. If you have a church home this should be one of the main things that are being taught, if not, find someone who can help you get to where you need to be. There are also spiritual tracts that can be very helpful.

A SCATTERED THOUGHT TO PONDER:

Are you sharing what you learn with others, and are you giving it your all?

The Power Is in Your Tongue

(Proverbs 18:21)

Speak Life, Not Death.

Proverbs is a book of Wisdom, but many refuse to read it; her pages are filled with knowledge. It is also a book that requires you to get help with; that is why God has given wisdom to others so that they would write, and we would understand.

It is perfectly okay to get you some other books that will help you to understand what the Word of God is saying. After all, we are to study to show ourselves approved unto God (2 Timothy 2:15). Investing is a good thing, and every Christian ought to do this.

Why would you want to lead or teach when you really are not prepared to do so, but it is happening? I am convinced that some people just like being in the limelight, be very careful in this area.

What you speak will come back to you, because the Word is before your very eyes (open your Bible and learn).

If you speak ill about your brother or sister, well, you have just cursed yourself. If you say you are sick, well then, you will be sick. If you speak about the man of God in a bad way, then you will be cursed. How sad it is that these things are happening every day, and we have all been guilty of it.

The enemy and his tactics are fooling people, causing them to think that it is God. Who called you to be so holy and to rule over your brothers and sisters? If you have that kind of power, then you should be helping and not being a hindrance. People who put themselves on a pedestal only set themselves up for a big fall.

When you carry yourself up the ladder, you will be coming back down, and it will not be the same way that you went up. We have been put here to love one another and speak blessings into the lives of others, and ourselves.

If you are not living the way that you know you should, you need to pray in your heart and ask God for forgiveness. He will, and He does constantly forgive us of all our sins.

The verse also says, they that love it shall eat the fruit thereof. As I have already forestated you can either be a blessing, or you can be a curse, it is all up to you. If you have the Holy Ghost ruling in your life then nothing is hard, just let Him have His way. He will lead you into all good things, so make it easy on yourself! After all, it's His job, remember, nothing is too hard for God, and it is never too late to change.

A Scattered thought to ponder:

Don't you know that what you speak will come back to you?

Disciple or Deserter

(1 John 1:7)

Jesus Is The Light

Walking in the Light of Jesus Christ brings us into fellowship with one another. Before you can have peace with your brother or sister; you must first come into fellowship with your Lord and Savior.

Could it be that is why some Christians cannot find peace with one another because they are not walking in the Light (Jesus)?

This Light, the Light of Jesus Christ will bring peace to any situation. It does not matter how grim it may seem to you; Jesus can and will fix it. But only if you allow Him to and stop yielding to your own will.

When we live in the Light of the Son of God, we find fellowship with Him to be easy. We are able to give Him glory, honor, and praise in the presence of others. Why? Because it comes, as some say natural, when it really is not, it is "The Spirit of the Lord." That is why we praise and adore Him for who He is, "He is the Light of the World."

As children of God, we have got to concentrate on always staying in this Light (Jesus).

There is nothing in darkness for a Christian; you should know this because you have been there too long. Yes, Lord, the truth be told, some of you are still there.

When the Light of Jesus shines on your wrong and reveals it to you, don't try to hold on to it, let it go.

Walking in the Light (Jesus) gives us an opportunity to respond to the Light (Jesus).

Your response should be thank you, Lord, for bringing me out, and for bringing me through, why? It is because you could not have done it without His Light (Jesus).

If you have true fellowship with God then you are walking in the Light, (Jesus) and you have been saved from your sins.

True fellowship with God came by the cross at Calvary, for you, and for me.

There is no other way; let the Light of Jesus shine inside of you.

He is the Light (Jesus) that will never go out.

He is the Light (Jesus) that shall never lose its power, yes, Jesus is Light.

A SCATTERED THOUGHT TO PONDER:

Aren't you tired of role-playing, and going through the motion of being a Christian?

Forgetting God

(Jeremiah 3:21-23)

The Backslider

Israel forgot God and fell into the worship of idols; nations are turning against Him even today.

But what about you, we have a personal relationship with the savior, and He is watching our every move?

Fact is, He is moving with you; everywhere you go.

Only a Christian can be a backslider.

Sinners just do what they do. They sin; it is their nature.

But you have to know that there is a better way.

He has freed you from your sins; He did not free you for you to go back, but He did it that you would keep going forward in your faith and following His holy will.

It is not a healthy thing to turn your back on God; it is serious, and it can be deadly for you.

The pleasures of this world are but for a moment; but eternity is forever.

Don't get caught up in the schemes of the unsaved, and the enemy.

They want nothing from you, but that you would come back out into the world with them.

You are supposed to be the stronger of the two; therefore, it is your job to pull them, not to be pulled.

This is their natural act, but it certainly should not be yours.

You are no longer a natural man; you are now a spiritual man.

The Word of God tells us to walk in the spirit, and not in the flesh, (John 3:6). When you gave your life to Christ, a change came with it; He is the best thing that ever happened to you. But you have got to see it for yourself, and you have to receive Him into your heart.

If you do not, it will not be effective at all; and it will not work.

When you are truly touched by the power of the Holy Ghost, you will change, and you will not be ashamed. You will want the world to know that you are born again and that you are happy that you are able to call on your Father in heaven. You can personally ask Him to help you in your time of weakness, and then you can be everything that He is calling you to be. God has forgiven you of your sins because He is a loving and compassionate God.

A SCATTERED THOUGHT TO PONDER:

Have you backslid? Do you know how to get back on track with God?

_____

_____

_____

Following but Not Really Understanding

(St. John 6:63-66)

Not A True Disciple

There are some people who are just going along for the ride. They find the things that Jesus says too hard to grasp; so they fall off. This is the same thing that they did when Jesus was here among them on the earth.

Jesus is the truth, and some can't handle it, so they close the book (The Bible) and run for the hills. When Jesus ascended back to the Father in heaven, He sent the Holy Ghost. He was poured out into the earth for all mankind (Salvation).

He came with life to give, and with life to be received by those who would believe in Jesus Christ. Jesus redeemed us by giving His life for us on the cross at Calvary.

He paid the ultimate price for all mankind. Now what you need to do is accept Him into your heart, believe that He is who He is (Jesus Christ) and confess your sins, and be saved.

This is what is happening in the world even now; man cannot understand Jesus because he is not in the right position to understand, some are still in their flesh, and the flesh cannot understand the ways of the Spirit. That is utterly impossible, and cannot be accomplished, without the Holy Ghost. The unsaved and unbelieving say that the Word of the Lord is hard to understand, well it is not, it is only hard for you because you are not saved and are not walking in the Spirit of the Lord.

The Holy Ghost is the one who shows you the way to the Father, through Jesus Christ, and, until you give your life to Him, you will never understand His ways, or His works. The Word of God says: You have blinders on your eyes; it is a veil that causes you not to see (2 Corinthians 3:13-15).

If you really want to see, come to Jesus; today would be a good day to do it, then your eyes will be opened. Jesus is waiting for you with open and loving arms!

A Scattered thought to ponder:

Are you ready to come to Jesus?

_____

_____

_____

Do Not Remember

(Isaiah 43:18-19)

Don't Do It

Jesus says, remember not the former things, neither consider the things of old, behold; I will do a new thing. Jesus will and He can, not man. Man can do nothing without the Lord.

This is a fact that man must face there are those who feel they are getting things done under their own power, but they are not! It is ludicrous even to think that you are.

Jesus tells us to remember that we have got to let go of past hurts and pains and look toward the future, where great things are awaiting us, and are in store just for us.

Jesus cannot use you holding on to your past, truthfully speaking; you are not even any good to your own self.

He tells us not to remember the things of old; what's done is done, and we cannot do anything about it.

But we can live for the moment that we are in.

Yes, there are those who do harbor and dwell on the things of the past.

They are people who sit up day in and day out thinking about who hurt them and who does not like them, get over it, if they didn't like the Savior of the world, then who are you supposed to be.

Learn to love yourself, and then you will be all right, until then you will always live in the past, in your mind.

God wants you to live for now, because tomorrow is not promised to any of us.

This is most important, living for Jesus; you are stronger than you think, and someone needs to see your strength.

Christian man and woman, don't you know that trials come to make you strong?

Don't be overcome by what you have already made it through, it's over, and it is behind you. Jesus is saying today, "I will do a new thing in you." The choice is yours. The question is, will you let Him?

A SCATTERED THOUGHT TO PONDER:

Will you allow Jesus to come into your life?

Inspired By My Brother In Christ

(2 Peter 1:7)

A Day in Prayer

This is my prayer for all of you, because as Jesus said, who is my brother or my sister?

Sometimes love is shared in strange ways, there are people who need to be needed, and there are also people who need to be loved.

Today I share the love of God with you, from my heart to yours.

May God continue to bless you throughout this day, in The Name of Jesus Christ our Lord and Savior!

May He give you the desires of your heart, as you walk obediently with Him!

May your family be covered in His love, may you have good health, blessed finances and the strength that can only come from depending on "Our Father, God"!

May all of your steps; be blessed with the favor of Almighty God.

May all who come into contact with you be blessed because of it!

May you continue to prosper in this "New Year" for every year that He gives to us is new, as well as every day!

There is nothing that can come upon you that He has not already taken care of, so be blessed is my prayer for you! To God is the glory for the things He is doing in all of your lives.

Amen.

A SCATTERED THOUGHT TO PONDER:

What do you need to turn over to Jesus?

_____

_____

_____

Spirit And Life

(John 6:53)

Jesus Said

"The words that I speak to you are spirit, and they are life." Nobody can speak as Jesus did, but we can be found doing our very best because of Him.

After Jesus ascended back to the Father in heaven, He sent the Holy Ghost into the world. The Holy Ghost will lead, guide, and show us the way, into all truth.

The Holy Spirit gives life (salvation) to all that will receive it.

You do know that everyone does not accept Him, right?

It saddens me to have to say it, but it is true.

Jesus has left us here to do a job in His holy name.

We are to remain obedient to Him to the very end of our very lives.

There is no price too great to pay for the life of a soul; Jesus has already paid it all.

Now we as Christians must go the distance and do all that we can in His holy name.

When a lost soul comes to Christ, we should all be ecstatic about it, because that is one less soul on its way to hell.

Nothing else is important as this even though some make it to be so.

It is past the time when we should be about our Father's business; there is a great harvest out there waiting, and it is ready to be picked.

Now, who will do this? If you are a Christian, you will.

Think about it, somebody witnessed to you, and you were born again; now it is your turn to be a witness for the Lord. You have your help; He is God the Holy Ghost!

He will stand with you, just as He stands for you.

If you have stepped out, or are on your way to doing so, you are in the will of God, and you are covered; His favor is with you.

Once you plant the seed your job is over, don't badger the person, then you get back and let the Holy Ghost do His job.

You can also give God the glory and the honor for using you, because He is Worthy, and it is in order.

A Scattered thought to ponder:

Who can you witness to?

Day and Night Word

(Joshua 1:8)

Meditate

The Word of God tells us we should meditate in His Word.

How often should we do this?

We should be in meditation every chance we get, day and night.

If you really have the Holy Ghost on the inside of you and you do.

If you have been saved, and I pray that you are, you will do just what He is commanding you to do.

We as Christians are to observe and to do according to all that is written in the Word of God, (the Bible) because when we do, we make our way prosperous.

Then and only then, will you have good success?

I don't know about you, but I love the thought of the promise that comes with this Word. Just look at it. God says, "We will do this!"

We will make our own way prosperous by being obedient to His holy will, isn't that awesome? You are at the wheel of your own prosperity you are the driver.

Give God the praise for showing you great and wonderful things.

He said to be a mediator of the Word of Almighty God.

There is nothing that you can do to top what the Lord God has already done.

There is no greater plan than that of *Our Father*. Hallelujah to your name, Lord God.

My Lord and My God, how excellent is thy name; *It Is So Excellent* that I will continue to meditate on it, day and night.

A SCATTERED THOUGHT TO PONDER:

So how can you get the blessings to come forth that are within you?

Become What His Word Say's

(St. Luke 4:17-21)

His Spirit Is Within Me

Jesus was no ordinary man; He was God in the flesh. Therefore, He could do whatever the Father wanted Him to do.

Isn't it amazing that the people of His time could hear what He read to them, and be in awe of what they heard, but could not accept Him for who He truly was!

There are people today who are the same way, they hear the "Spoken Word," but they cannot accept what they hear.

There are some people who just do not want to give up their old ways because they feel they are really living; they think, and they feel; that that are really the good life.

I can remember the time when I was in that same mode of thinking; but; the more I got into the Word, the more it got into me.

I appeal to you today, if this sounds at all like you, or if you have a friend or know someone living such a life, pray for him or her.

Pray that they will come to their senses before it is everlasting too late.

There is no shame in genuine repentance, only freedom.

Jesus said to them that favor was before them, that favor was Himself, God Incarnate, (in the flesh).

He has blessed us with His Word, and with His grace, what else do you need?

How long will you continue down the road that only leads to destruction in the end?

He is the Lord of Lord's and King of Kings.

He loves you and wants to be your Savior and Lord. He is giving to you this day healing and a new way of life.

You have to trust the Holy Ghost to lead you and guide you.

A Scattered thought to ponder:

If Jesus depended on the Spirit for empowerment, what does that say to you?

Where Is Your Treasure?

(Matthew 6:20)

Do You Have Any?

The Word of God tells us to "Store up our treasures in heaven, where neither moth nor rust destroys, and where thieves do not break in or steal."

This gives me great joy, to know that I have a Father who loves me so much, that He has prepared a place for me, to store up my good deeds.

A place where no man can enter and rob, or steal; it won't decay, it cannot be destroyed, that is truly wonderful.

I know of no place on earth where this could happen.

Just as an example: We have stuff stored in warehouses, valuables stored in banks; some even hide things in their homes, but to no avail, because stuff always gets destroyed, in some way or another.

For instance, fires destroy homes where you have hidden things, people rob banks, and those clothes that you can't wear anymore, but won't let go of, the moth over the years destroy them.

Have you ever went into your closet and pulled something out that has been hanging there for years and see little holes that were not there when you first put it in the closet? That is a reminder from God that you have stored up in the wrong place, those little destroyers that we cannot see are called moth.

We must store our treasures in the right place. Truly God did not leave us without instruction concerning everything that we do or say.

You cannot see what He is saying with your physical eyes; you must learn how to use your spiritual eyes.

You can only do this by staying in the Word of God; you should also be receiving good teaching and preaching from your Pastor.

Growth becomes imperative when you follow the guidelines of the Father.

When you are carnal minded (flesh), you will operate in spiritual darkness.

Come out of your spiritual darkness, and into His marvelous light. You will be glad that you did.

Do that which is pleasing to the Father (in your spirit), and not that which is pleasing to man (in your flesh).

A Scattered thought to ponder:

What can you do that would be pleasing to Jesus?

The Little Man

(St. Luke 19:4)

Rejoice

Sometimes we can be too high for our own good, even though we may mean well by it, or we feel that we just don't size up, as did Zacchaeus.

Jesus does not see us by statute, or by merit; you may be one who has accomplished a lot in your lifetime.

But it does not matter one iota if Jesus is not a part of your life.

We need to be a Zacchaeus, when he could not get results, he climbed higher; he got up in a tree so that he could see Jesus.

Jesus already knew him, and called him by his name, does He know you?

Do you know Him?

Zacchaeus was so happy when Jesus noticed him out of the whole crowd.

Jesus told him to come down, and that He was going to His house.

This pleased Zacchaeus very much that he welcomed Jesus. We should be ecstatic when Jesus calls us out!

Has Jesus been invited to your home yet, does He have permission to dwell there every day, and is He welcome?

When you are saved and walking by faith, your attitude should be that of joy at all times. It does not matter what comes your way, or who comes to bother you.

Jesus is all you will ever need, let Him in.

Do you know that your body is the temple of the Holy Ghost?

Therefore, your home should be a holy place; it should be a place where you find peace, and others can come in and feel that same peace when they enter your door.

Zacchaeus was not a saved man when Jesus called Him out of that tree, but after His visit with Jesus, things changed.

He was no longer a crooked tax collector, and he wanted to give back to the poor and pay back fourfold what he owed.

He wanted the people to know that having a life with Jesus will change you.

If you have not changed and say that you are saved, then it is a possibility that you are not saved!

You need to repent of your sins and come back to the Lord. He will take you back; He never turns away those that He loves, because you are His.

It does not matter what you do, someone is going to always talk out loud, and under his or her tongue; but you keep on doing what you know is right.

People are placed in position by how those in authority feel about them in today's world. But thanks are to God that He does not work that way, He sees every work and every good deed that you do. So, don't stop working because of man; keep on going, for your reward is ahead of you.

A SCATTERED THOUGHT TO PONDER:

Do you feel undervalued?

_____

_____

Sowing Seed and Reaping A Harvest

(Ecclesiastes 11:4-6)

It Shall Come To Pass

We have no control over the things of the future, but we do have a blessed opportunity to be partakers of all that God has in store for us.

We have to do our part in order to receive the blessings of God.

He has told us that we are to sow, that my friend is a done deal.

Some people are sowing without even knowing it; as a matter of fact, you have been sowing all of your life, but you need to know that, there is a better way.

We need to sow according to the "Word of God."

He says that you shall reap what you sow, this is true, and you will before you leave this earth.

I believe that you know for a fact that this is true in your life, whether you are Christian or Non - Christian.

If you have mistreated someone in life, you yourself have been mistreated.

If you cheated in any way, you too, have been cheated.

I could go on and on, but I won't, you know exactly where this fits you.

You need to be an active – positive person in the name of Jesus.

You can sow good seeds in the lives of your loved ones and others.

There is so much you can do in His name, if you only would.

Solomon reminds us that we cannot see the wind, but we feel it upon our faces.

We see the crops grow that are planted because of the rain which waters the earth, at the right time.

We cannot see the forming of the bones of an infant in the womb of his mother, but it is happening, and eventually, after nine months, we see the results.

When we look upon that newborn baby, in the arms of the mother; we cannot see all of the mighty works that God has performed, and yet they do exist.

Our duty as children of God; is to walk in faith and believe.

We should sow to God for the things that we want to come to pass in our lives, and the lives of our loved ones, and others.

Nobody can do it but God, okay?

We are to keep on sowing; Solomon lets us know that we don't know from where it will come, and from what source of sowing that we have done.

But we have surety in knowing that it is coming; that is God's promise to us.

If you have not been sowing, now would be a good time to start.

Start by sowing seeds of kindness, then sow into some well-established ministry, sow into your church, sow into your pastor, and sow into the lives of others.

Sow out of obedience because it is the Word of God.

A Scattered thought to ponder:

What are you trusting God for?

_____

_____

_____

I Believe God

(Acts 27:23-25)

Enough Said

As you go through life, you will face many trials, and go through many storms, but you must hold on to your faith.

We are all tested each and every day; it is nothing that you cannot overcome, trust Jesus to bring you through.

God has your angel right there beside you; He is steering you through every situation that befalls you.

You have to see (envision) Him for yourself.

You have the Holy Ghost on the inside of you; He is here to lead and guide you into all truth if you let Him.

Let go of those reins, because they do not belong to you anymore, and follow God!

You cannot be helped unless you allow Him to do what He is there to do. He is your protector.

Trust God all the time, not just some of the time. He is your heavenly Father.

Sometimes you can feel as though the things of the world are overtaking you; but believe me when I tell you, that God is ever present, and He knows everything that you are going through.

He has set things before us to make us strong; we will never grow if we don't experience some things in this life.

Some do nothing but complain, but I say; stop complaining, and live each day as if it were your last.

There are those who are going through way more than you and handling it very well.

Get with a strong brother or sister in Christ, where you can pull on their strength, and be encouraged by them.

Take the advice of Paul, and be happy in whatever state (control your mind) you are in.

God has already gone before you; He has done so to make sure that you will be all right when you do finally arrive at that point of your life. There is nowhere you are going that the Lord has not already been, got it. God is a God of His Word, and He never fails (that is assurance). He is God, and He has got it like that, trust Him.

A SCATTERED THOUGHT TO PONDER:

Do you trust God to do what He said He would do?

Godly Goals

(1 Corinthians 9:24-27)

Simply Amazing

In order to receive what God has for you, there are some things that have to be done; there are some changes that have to be made, and there are some things that you have to give up.

If you want to receive His crown, you must, do what He requires of you. There are people today who wear crowns; made by the hands of man these will not last. But, the crown that Paul is speaking of, it will last throughout eternity. It is a crown given by Jesus Christ, a crown that no one can take from you. It is a crown that you will never have to relinquish, (give up).

As a child of God, you must be conditioned for this journey through life, it will not be an easy one, but, if you train and condition yourself, you will make it. Self-discipline is a good thing; it is something that a spirit-filled person needs to practice, every day!

But, as a Christian, it is your choice; "The Lord" will not force you to do anything. Paul shows us how this works first hand; He went through extensive training, like that of an athlete, to get to where he was.

Christians should have goals; it should be something that drives you, something that keeps you moving toward the mark of the high calling of Christ Jesus.

The greatest thing that we could ever do is preparing ourselves to be soul winners for our Lord and Savior Jesus Christ.

He has given you this opportunity to do all that you possibly can in His name.

Don't you be a quitter, because a quitter never wins; trust Jesus, and you will make it?

Just make sure that while you are preaching to others, that you get what you need to so that the Lord God does not reject you.

After all, He is the one who holds your life and mine in the palm of His hand.

So, remember that obedience is always better than sacrifice. If God has given you something to do, and He has, do it with every fiber of your being.

A word of caution to the hardheaded: God is still the Master Disciplinarian - past, present, and future. There is no getting around Him. You should not even want to.

A Scattered thought to ponder:

Are you obedient?

_____

_____

_____

Watch Out for Those Snakes In Your Life

(Acts 28:3-5)

They Are Present

You need to be absolutely sure that the blood of Jesus covers you. Have you given your life to Christ?

If not what in this world are you waiting on? Tomorrow is not promised to you, and there is too much going on in this world for you to be winging it, and not have His covering over your life.

Paul is one of the greatest examples that we could ever have in the Word of God; we can certainly learn how we should live from his life experiences.

He was one of the greatest Christians that ever lived; he was also according to God's Word, the greatest persecutor that ever lived.

It is truly amazing how a life can be changed when one finds his way?

There are people around you now, who do not need to be. I'm stepping out here on the Word of God, and you may not like it, but the Word of God is true, and it will make you free, (St. John 8:32). You definitely know that a snake is a cold-blooded creature, and you also know that he has no problem striking when the opportunity presents itself.

Everybody does not love you; and everybody is not your friend, okay.

It makes no difference what you are doing for them, or with them.

Allow yourself to have some down time away from everyone, and some up time with the Lord Jesus.

This is one of the things that is lacking in the lives of most Christians.

If you always need to have an audience and be in the presence of others, this is not good. The best audience you can, or will ever have, is when you go before your Father in heaven.

How "Awesome" it is that you have the Father, Son, and The Holy Ghost.

When you've got Jesus, you don't have to worry about the bite or the venom.

You don't even have to be concerned about the swelling, because there will be none.

If you put your total trust in the Lord; who is your healer, so give Him the glory, for protecting you, from all of your enemies great and small.

A Scattered thought to ponder:

Are you holding on to a snake? Why can't you let them go? What is it that is causing you to hold on to them, or who is it?

The Attributes of God

(Genesis 1 – Revelation 22)

He Is All Of This!

He is God Infinite: We cannot limit or understand him as we do with a <u>finite man</u>, (human). God spoke everything into existence, except man.

His name "I AM THAT I AM," is the first name mentioned to Moses in the Old Testament.

He is God Self-Existing: God is God, He is a person, and He is not connected to anything or anyone in order to exist.

He is God Triune: God is three persons in one, God the Father, God the Son and God the Holy Ghost. He is the God that you should accept and come to know as your personal Lord and Savior.

He is God Transcendent: Heaven is His home, and the earth where we live is His footstool. Nothing that we relate too in the earth can describe our God.

I see Him as "Totally Awesome"! We were made for Him and for His pleasure.

God is too high to be reached in the physical state of man. But He can be reached in the Spirit [God the Holy Ghost] if you are saved.

He is God Immanent: God dwells within us (God the Holy Ghost), He is every-where present. You may not accept Him as your Savior and Lord, but you certainly know that He is real and that He is God. God is spiritual and not material, that is what He desires for all who follow Him; He desires us to live our lives in the Spirit of the Lord.

He is *God Omniscient:* He is all knowing, the past, the present, and the future are in His hands.

He is God the Truth (Holy Spirit), He knows all about you and your life.

He knows every move that you are going to make before you make it.

He is God Sovereign: He is all power, and all power is in His hands, It Is He who rules and Super rules. Everything is under His control, even the devil and his demons; there is only so much that he is allowed to do.

He is God Is Love: because He gave His only Son for us, this is the true love. The Lord wants to have an intimate relationship with you, He is the Father, and He loves you.

He is God Holy: Holy, holy, holy is the Lord God Almighty, praise Him for His holiness all the people of the Lord.

A Scattered thought to ponder:

Who is God to you?

_____

_____

_____

Moving by The Power Of God

(James 2:22)

Through Faith

Everything that lives and moves does so by the power of Almighty God.

We can do nothing through self-will; all that we do is by His power.

It does not matter what your race, religion, or age is, you move, by His power.

It is past the time for people to stop the madness of being ignorant as to whom God is.

It is a sinful shame that you have a Creator who you refuse to acknowledge, and trust.

There is a day coming when you will give Him the glory that He deserves.

There is a day coming when you will confess and bow to His holy Name.

All man was created for God; not for your own purposes, the enemy has tricked you.

You were created to praise Him and Him only.

As children of God we must hold on to our faith, and we must put it into action.

These two go together like peas in a pot.

Faith is fulfilled in action.

Example: Paul said that Abraham was justified by his faith (Romans 4:3).

James said that Abraham was justified by faith in what he did, (James 2:23). James took it even farther after he said this. He also said that Abraham became the friend of God.

It is an honor to be called the friend of God; however, you will never reach this status in your unbelief.

I want to encourage you today to stop being led by your own little mind and by the influence of those who are around you, who choose not to believe, and obey.

A SCATTERED THOUGHT TO PONDER:

What has God told you to do in faith that you haven't done?

_____

_____

_____

My Birth Date

(Matthew 9:29)

Verification

Every man, woman, boy, and girl has a special day; it is called a birthday, or as some may say the day you were born. God chose the date that you were to arrive on the earth before you were placed in your Mother's womb. He knows exactly how to spark our interest if we would just listen.

Now that you have been well informed you can really read His Word! According to the scripture that relates to my date of birth, Jesus was followed by two blind men they were men to whom he restored their sight.

I said that to say this, it is no coincidence to me that this story is about blind men; I find it to be truly amazing, as a matter of fact, I can really relate to it.

My mother before she went to heaven lost her sight to some kind of sickness; we really never knew exactly what it was. I had two cousins who lost their sight in their later years to diabetes (both are in heaven now). But what I really want you to get is this: as a teenager, I had a recurring dream, or really a vision, that God kept before me.

I would always see myself, it was just like watching the television, and each time I had this vision I saw myself blind; keep following me now.

I was blind, but I could see, this is the truth; it was the strangest thing I had ever encountered.

I would see like it was foggy white or on a grayscale. I know that God was warning me and getting me ready for what was coming down the road. You see God will never let anything slip upon you. He will always prepare you for it. I believe this with all of my heart. I thank God that I was already in His Word, learning and growing daily.

Years later (it was back in the late 1980s), I was watching the TV, when I heard the Holy Ghost speak and say to me, "Put your hand over your left eye." I thought it strange, but I did it. That very instant, I realized that I could not see very well out of my right eye.

To make a long story short; after calling and going to my eye doctor and being ushered from there to several eye specialists, it was determined that I had a twenty-five percent loss of sight. But to the amazement of the doctors and others, I can still see out of my right eye, and it is exactly as I described it to you in my vision. I give God the glory, the honor, and the praise for my sight; because it is certainly nothing that I did, nor the doctors. God is, certainly and without a doubt, the Master healer; He is *Jehovah Rapha*. If you believe in "The Lord Jesus" it will come to pass. We praise you, Oh God, Amen.

A SCATTERED THOUGHT TO PONDER:

What dream has God given you to believe?

_____

_____

_____

Will You Be Ready When Jesus Comes?

(St. Matthew 24:44)

I Hope So

It is important that we keep our minds focused on the Lord and stay alert.

You cannot get good instruction anywhere but in the Word, and by The Holy Ghost.

The reason that we are to stay alert is; that we do not know when or where the Lord is going to appear.

One thing that Scripture assures us of is; that, He is coming back again.

He is coming back for His bride, (the church).

It is a true fact that we never know when a thief may come, but Jesus does.

His Word prepares us for any thief and any attack; that may or will come our way.

That is why you need to live in it, and by it; "His Word" it is our refuge and our strength.

We need always to stay prayed up so that we do not lose our strength because our strength is in the Lord.

We are living in a day and time when things are just not what they appear to be.

We see, and we hear of so much crime. We see and hear of terrible sinful acts; acts against innocent little children and even against ourselves. It is just sickening.

If you don't have Jesus Christ in your life, then you are already a loser.

People may, as they say, be enjoying themselves now, but it will not last.

You will without a shadow of a doubt have to face the man who died for you, the man who gave His life for you, "Jesus Christ."

A believer needs to always be on the alert so that nothing will be able to slip upon you. God has given us an assurance in His Word; that the saints of God are going to be all right, and that is "Good News."

It is truly wonderful to know that the Lord has us in His loving protection, so why not celebrate Him today? He is worthy of your praise.

A Scattered thought to ponder:

There is no getting by Him or around Him; my question to you is why would you even want too?

Please Answer Me Oh Lord

(Psalm 69:16)

God Will Answer You

God really does have a sense of humor.

I made a commitment to go before the Lord in prayer starting this morning at a certain time, for the next thirty days.

I was laying there in my warm bed somewhere in my thoughts between woke and sleep. I finally decided to open my eyes and look at the clock.

All I could do was smile and say, "God, you really do have a sense of humor." When I looked at the clock, it had exactly six o clock.

My commitment time is 6:00 – 7:00 AM; get it.

I believe that God takes us more seriously when we say that we are going to do something and write it down. Why would I say this?

I came upon a journal that I had received for Christmas of 2005 from my Mother-in-law, Ms. Dorothy Adams.

On January 26, 2006, I was moved by the Holy Spirit to write down what I heard being spoken to me.

What I heard the Lord saying to me was this: That I would write a book.

Well, what can I say the proof is in your hand, and you are reading it?

This is how God works with me; I have been listening to Him for a long time.

I have also been penning the Word of God for over twenty years, or more, but it was out of what I called, I just like to write, and have notes available to me for further use.

I could not understand why when I first began to write, but now I know.

It was a vision that has been made plain, and it now lives because of my obedience to God.

All of the glory, the honor, and the praise, are to Him.

I am nothing but an instrument of His holy will; and a grateful one at that, because I know the Favor of the Lord is upon me.

The Lord has placed a gift or gifts in all of us; this may be your day to discover what that gift is.

A Scattered thought to ponder:

What have you committed to doing in writing?

_____

_____

_____

From Revelation to Reality

(Hebrews 11:32-39; 2 Peter 1:4)

He Is So Real

The Author speaks of the Old Testament heroes in this chapter of Hebrews.

Through faith in Jesus God accepts us; it is our faith that makes us whole.

It is our faith that heals us and delivers us into the hands of "All Sovereign God."

His Word tells us that without faith it is impossible to please God (Hebrews 11:6). That is awesome within itself; faith is an important factor in the life of a Christian.

We have been in the revelation of things a long time; it is now time to step into the reality of it.

If you really believe in God, then now is the time to let Him have His way, in your life. Easton's Bible Dictionary defines Revelation "it is the supernatural communication of truth to the mind; inspiration secures to the teacher or writer infallibility in communicating that truth to others. It renders its subject the spokesman or prophet of God in such a sense that everything he asserts to be true, whether fact or doctrine or moral principle, is true, infallibly true.

It is a truth that has been told down through generations and generations of people, and it will continue to be told as long as there is life on the earth.

Until Jesus comes back the saints of God will voice it.

Reality is the quality or state of being real, and it is time that we are real, first with God, others, and then self. God has given us His promises that He certainly does keep, they are precious, and they are great.

So is your faith, faith comes from God and is very precious in His sight. Now, we must get busy and do the things we have been called to do for they are for an appointed time. He has given us gifts, gifts that can only be used for the purpose of Kingdom building, so what are you doing with yours?

He has His eye on you, so be very careful and do not anger Him by wasting that which He has blessed you with.

There is an inheritance awaiting you, at the return of Jesus Christ; and then you shall receive your just reward if you have been faithful to His calling on your life.

A Scattered thought to ponder:

Do you know what calling is on your life?

God's Oracles

(Romans 3:2; 1 Peter 4:11; Hebrews 5:12)

The Utterances of God!

He is a speaker for the Lord and an orator of the Logos Word.

Christian service has two categories:

Principle One - Teach

This is good to know because we have Christians who want to just jump up and go for it.

They think that they don't have to be taught, they feel that they know it all.

Well, it is time to set the record straight; it is not about me, my, or I, and it is not about education or non-education, even though having an education does help us to understand much better.

God's desire is that we learn of Him before we go out trying to teach someone else the way. Become acquainted with the Father before trying to spout off about Him.

The way that we learn is to stay connected to the Holy Ghost; He is our teacher.

He is the one that will lead you into all truth.

Principle Two – Serve

Everyone has not been called to lead.

Someone has to be a servant, and which is the greater of the two?

If you rely on God's Word and strength, through Jesus Christ in what you do, it is God who wins.

Why? Because Jesus Christ is the Logos of God: (St. John 1:1-4, 14). That is Word.

All glory and praise belong to God, and at no time will God share His glory with us.

If you are doing what you are doing for selfish purposes, you are already on the losing end, and you already have received your reward.

We ought to be like Peter and recognize and honor God for who He truly is. He is Sovereign God; and I will say as Peter has said, "Amen."

A Scattered thought to ponder:

Do you know God's word? Do you rely on it?

_____

_____

_____

He Said It

(Revelation 19:9)

That's Enough For Me

John was commanded to record this message; blessed are those who are invited to the wedding supper of the Lamb.

God has a different program designed for each group of saints, which corresponds to the relationship to His overall program.

Here the church described as His bride, will be attended by the angels and by saints.

I believe that is why the Church of God is almost at its peak.

We see the blessings of the Lord every time we enter His house.

The wedding supper relates to the second coming of Christ.

Therefore, the wedding supper according to God's Word has not yet taken place.

Jesus Christ has not yet come the second time, but He shall indeed come, and when He comes again, He is coming in all of His glory.

We are still at this time in the age of soul saving, and soul winning.

It is happening everywhere, all over the world, and it is not happening by chance; it is the will of God. There are people coming to Christ at all ages, and it is not coincidental that these things are happening.

It is by the Word of God that people are being saved in such a phenomenal way. It is a supernatural act of the Lord God Almighty and through those whom He has chosen.

We know that there will be a time when these things shall be no more. That is why we have to be aggressive in our witness to the people of the world who are not yet saved.

God is a good God; He's giving everyone a chance to be saved, and it is most definitely up to the individual to make the right choice.

When the opportunity presents itself and it will; I pray that you will not be one who refuses the chance to be saved from all of your sins and have an eternal home in glory.

As the angel has said, these are the true Words of God.

A Scattered thought to ponder:

Are you actively winning souls?

If You Want to See God Look Up

(Psalm 40:2)

God Has No Image

The human eye with all of creation points cannot see God in His existence.

Jesus has testified to His existence, and His desire to be sought by His creatures.

He also provided us with an example of how to live our lives, seeking and serving God. A lot of our troubles are brought about by our own sins, but God is still a God of mercy and compassion. If you trust God, He will bring you through, and He will bring you out.

A lot of you are putting your own selves down, beating your own selves up, and etc. Do you really think that God needs your help in punishing you?

No, He certainly does not!

You cannot keep your head down and expect to see the Lord.

The world is full of beautiful reminders of His presence; the birds are singing and flying through the air, that's just one of many put your mind to work positively and see what you come out with.

Oh, the many things a man will do in the flesh, things that will bring nothing but harm to himself. The spirit man does not function in that way, because the Spirit of the Lord leads him.

So please my brother and sister, don't give control of your life to others; people love to control you, and they do it because you let them. You have got to stop relinquishing your power to the enemy, (Satan); stop letting him control you in your thoughts and actions. Stop it right now; stop letting him beat you up one side; and down the other.

Pull yourself up out of that state of depression, and oppression.

The Holy Ghost is always there. He is waiting on you to yield your life to Him; He does not have a choice, because you are the one who chooses how your life will go, and where. The Holy Ghost has been waiting for you to let go and let Him have all of that mess. The reason is that you will never get yourself together on your own.

I want to assure you now, that if you yield your will to Him; you will have no regrets that you did. Why fight a battle that does not belong to you? Your battle belongs to the Lord; and yes, He can, and certainly will handle it.

A SCATTERED THOUGHT TO PONDER:

Will you yield yourself to God?

Working, But Not Out of Love

(Psalm 28:5)

Be Very Careful

It is not good to get caught up in your work. There is a difference in what *you* consider important versus what *God* deems important.

We should always petition the Lord about what we should be doing, and about the way, it is to be done, and the when, where and how it is to be done, after all, who knows better than the Lord God?

We should always be willing to wait for instruction, no matter how long it may seem to take, because every time we decide to get something done without the Lord, we only make it worse.

Then we have to come back to Him repent of the sin and ask the Holy Ghost for His guidance.

We must also be willing to forgive others as we are forgiven.

We must also work toward a better prayer life.

It is not enough for us to pray every now and then; or to meet the Lord on Sunday morning, and Wednesday nights, it won't work.

That will only leave you with feelings of guilt if you are real in your walk.

God requires all of us to work; therefore, we are to work even at getting better.

It is also His desire that we trust and depend on Him; that should be our desire to, whom else can you trust.

How can you do this if you never call upon Him for guidance and encouragement?

When we allow the Lord to have His way in our life, it will only make things better.

I learned a long time ago about trying to do things on my own.

Take a look at your life; is it pleasing in His sight, be honest with you!

Are you working the works of the Lord? Or are you just going through the motions, where people will leave you alone? Who are you in the market of pleasing, God or man?

I hope and pray that it is for the Lord because if it is not, your work is in vain.

It is a true fact that man can reward you, but it is a reward that will soon perish and fade away so why not choose the work of the Lord and receive a just reward.

You may be pleased with where you are right now, but this is not becoming of a Christian. Being Christ-like demands a change in your work ethics. God has great things in store for you. He has higher levels that He wants to take you to, but He cannot if you will not submit to *His* will and *His* way.

It does not matter where you work; or who you are working for, just be aware of the fact that God has placed you there to make the difference, and to make a change, by the life you are now living in Him.

A Scattered thought to ponder:

How often do you pray? Do you feel it is effective?

_____

_____

_____

Abraham, Father of Faith

(Romans 4:16)

Chosen by God

You can only receive the promise of God by faith; the law has nothing to do with faith in God.

His promise also comes by faith to all who are the children of Abraham; it is a promise from Almighty God.

This promise is not just to the Jews, but it is also to the Gentiles, it is for everyone who will exercise their faith in God, and it does not come by circumcision, because circumcision cannot save you.

Abraham is the father of all who believe in the promise of God.

If you do not believe by faith in God, then He is not your Father (Galatians 3:29).

Abraham was justified not because he worked for it, but because he trusted God.

The promise of blessings is given to those whom God has imputed as righteous, but it is still connected to your faith.

God blessed Abraham because of his obedience, (Genesis 22:18) and He will and can do the same for you.

There are two connecting factors in this Word. They are Faith and Grace; these two go together.

Faith is yours to do. It is yours to stir up, move in, and live by every day of your life.

It was by faith that Abraham believed God, his faith declared his righteousness.

Grace comes from God, it is His Unmerited favor, and His grace is upon all mankind, it is free.

His grace is sufficient, for those who will receive it, God's grace is the best gift that any man could ever reach out and take hold of, and yet It is the one blessed gift that man has turned his back on.

It is the ultimate gift, of His undying love, for all mankind.

A SCATTERED THOUGHT TO PONDER:

What about you? How is your faith?

Does What You Are Doing Line Up?

(1 Peter 2:9-10)

With the Word of God

We have been chosen by God to live a life before Him and the world that is pleasing in His sight.

We are His Royal priest, we are a holy nation, or should be, we belong to Him. He has lifted us out of our sins, into His marvelous light.

Is the life that you are living a respectful one before Him, or are you doing everything that pleases you? When the Holy Ghost came into your life, a change came with Him.

If you are still doing the things of the flesh, then you have not yet yielded your will to the will of the Father.

A Christian should practice holiness every day; because holiness is not something that you do only on Sunday's at morning worship, holiness is a lifestyle.

It is time that you begin to live your life in the beauty of His holiness.

Jesus Christ died on the cross so that you would be able to do just that.

There used to be a very popular saying among the Christians, it really grew, and made millions of dollars; everywhere that you looked, you would see it, and I quote "what would Jesus do"?

I am sure that you have heard it and even spoken it yourself. I have given you the answer to the question, it is cut and dry, and it is finished, He died for you, and He is not going to do it again.

You do not have to stay on that path of destruction; you have been saved and sanctified (set apart), by the Lord.

When you live a life that is Spirit-filled (Holy Ghost), there will be no regrets, because it brings joy and peace! But, when you continue to live a life of sin and do what you want to do, you will never be happy.

Why? Because the Holy Ghost is inside of you. He is there to lead and guide you into all things. He is waiting for you to surrender the reins of your life to Him. You should be regrettably tired by now from all those spiritual wrecks you have encountered.

If you are a crooked Christian, a backslider, a gambler, an adulterer, fornicator, and the list goes on. Just ask God's forgiveness, and then straighten up and go on.

Yes, we are special, because God has reserved us for Himself and for the sole purpose of praising and adoring Him all day long. Hallelujah to the God of God; and Lord of Lord, Amen

A Scattered thought to ponder:

What would Jesus do?

An Unusual Request

(Joshua 10:8; 12; 14)

One Man Prayer

When God delivers it's a done deal; the Lord God was awfully good to Joshua and his men, the victory was theirs because God said it was done, Joshua could be very confident in that fact.

He knew that the break he needed was now his for the taking.

When God is blessing you, you do not need to deviate from what He is telling you to do, and the reason is; that it could and will result in your being on the loosening end. We need to always praise Him for His mighty acts; which are happening every day.

Can you not see God working in your life, and the lives of your family, church family, and friends, oh yes, and even the lives of your enemies. How many times has God stood up for you? And you never gave it a second thought, as a matter of fact, you never even remembered to say thank you.

God really does bless us, because He loves us; and He wants us to see Him in every situation of our lives.

With the presence of the Lord God in your life, you never have to be afraid. He is your battle fighter. He is the one who causes our enemies to fall.

What you need to do my brother's and my sister's is, to trust Him, and to hold on to His Unchanging Hand.

Joshua prayed to God for what He needed, and God in His Infinite Wisdom answered Joshua right away, Oh God how Awesome you are.

His request was one that most of us would never have been able even to think up, let alone do.

Now, if Joshua could ask God for more daylight and be blessed with his request; what do you think He will do for you, right now?

This I believe is one of the most powerful prayers that have ever been prayed. God stopped the sun and the moon at Joshua's request.

To pray in faith results in great miracles; God Himself supernaturally does that.

Joshua prayed at noontime; that lets us know that prayer is always in order and should be done at all times, it is not meant for us to pray that one prayer, just before you go to bed, as some so easily do.

Prayer should be uttered all day long, and it matters not where you are when you pray, because, your prayers, comes from within you.

A SCATTERED THOUGHT TO PONDER:

What do you dare ask God for?

Master Publisher

(Psalm 68:1; 11)

God Gave The Word

When God moves, His enemies (which are our enemies) are no longer a threat.

It does not matter whether you are dealing with them in the flesh or in the spirit.

The power of God is the overwhelming mover and shaker of all evil.

God gave the Word; He had already declared that He would be victorious over the Canaanite kings (Exodus 23:22-23).

He is still giving the same Word today because His Word does not change.

All through the Bible, you can find where the people of God fought and won because God was their protector.

He was there with them in Egypt and in the wilderness.

He bought them out, and as they went, He went before them.

God is still going before His people even today.

The Holy Ghost is real, He is God, and He is the third in The Godhead.

All you need to do is trust and believe Him to bring you through.

God has always moved on those who believe in Him; He has inspired people from the beginning of time.

He has made sure that His Word was always reachable for those who would receive it. His Word is our strength in the time of storm; for truly the storms of life are still raging.

God is always giving inspiration to those who will hear it.

If you have been saved and are living a right life, listen for the voice of God.

You may not be saved, but the same applies to you.

He said in the day you hear His voice, harden not your heart (Hebrews 4:7).

Yes, God is here, and this just might be your blessed day to hear and obey.

A Scattered thought to ponder:

Has your heart become hardened?

_____

_____

_____

Our Gracious God

(Psalm 67:1-7)

The Blessings of God

The people of God praised God because of His goodness.

God is a righteous God; He judges us fairly and accordingly.

There is no one alive, or who has ever lived, that can say, God has judged them unfairly. God gives divine approval to those who follow and obey Him (He made His face to shine upon them).

In other words, if you stay in His holy will, you will receive His favor upon your life.

Favor is awesome because it goes beyond you all the way to the throne of God.

When God's favor comes upon you, you are able to pass that favor on to others.

There is or may be someone around you right now who is not saved, you can be the instrument by which they are if you would just speak into their lives the way of salvation.

I just cannot understand how people go from day to day with friends who are not saved, and they never ever witness to them...why?

What is it that you are afraid of?

Someone helped you; now it is your turn to do the same!

We are always to give God praise, because He truly is worthy.

There is no room in the life of a Christian, for so-called shame, or I don't want to lose them.

What about the fact that they may be lost forever if you don't speak?

You should want people to know that you are a strong Christian in the Lord.

It is good medicine for those that are around you, and it is good for you too.

It will bring spiritual growth into your life, but in order to get there you have to stay in the Word of God and let His Word get in you, then you will be one that He can and will use.

Yes, it is true that people really do like to tease those that are strong in their convictions, well guess what?

I see that as I wish I had what you have and could do what you do.

Jealousy is still alive and will continue to be one of the things that you will have to deal with as a Christian.

When you bless God He will give you a bountiful harvest; it's His Word.

The earth will even be fruitful for you.

Isn't that awesome? The increase will be yours.

That in itself should give you joy; but most of all, just knowing who God is and what He has blessed you with should be absolutely enough.

A Scattered thought to ponder:

Are you blessing God? How?

_____

_____

_____

Because Of His Mercy

(Psalm 56:4)

No Fear

There is no need at all to have a fear of another human being, but we do!

Some men and women can be and are dangerous beings, all because they depend and trust in the wrong things and wrong spirits.

There are people being killed and tormented each and every day at the hands of evil people.

It is happening in our schools, churches, homes, along the highways of life and on and on.

Good people leave home going to work or wherever, and they never return alive.

That my friend; is the work of the enemy, the devil, (Satan). This you have to know it is vital to your well-being.

God is saying to us, if you trust in me, I will bless you I will protect you from all hurt, harm, and danger.

It is imperative that you get into the Word of God and live your life accordingly.

How can you praise His Word if you don't know His Word (Jesus Christ)?

David was a very smart man. He put his trust where it counted the most, he trusted in God.

When your enemies come against you, turn them over to the Lord. You are no match for what is really going on. You see the person the individual; but God sees the foul spirit that it is, for what it is, and what it is trying to do, to your life.

God is All Power; He has control over everyone and everything.

Evil people can cause unrest in your life, but God the Father is the one who will restore you.

How am I restored? I am restored because of His Mercy, and His Grace.

Therefore, I can boldly say The Lord is my help and I will not fear what man will do to me (Hebrews 13:6).

Because of this I now know that my prayer life, my beliefs, and my faith in Him, will never be shattered.

To God are the glory, the honor, and the praise.

A Scattered thought to ponder:

Do you fear man? Why or why not?

Forever God

(Psalm 48:1; 10; Psalm 121:3)

Even To Death

God is an ever-present God; He is our strength and our help.

He shelters us from the dangers of this world. We find our shelter by trusting in our Father. He is so good to us. He looks down on us, and is merciful, in all of His glory. He never sleeps. He never gets tired. He never stops loving and watching over us.

What good news this should be to all the saints of God.

There are many things that can and will come against you, but as a child of God, you are not to worry or be afraid.

You need to always put your trust in the Lord, and He will do the rest.

That is His job He does not need us getting in His way.

He has given us plenty to do in His Word and learn of Him.

Do not even try to do the Lord's work; all you are going to do is fail.

When you get into that mode of thinking and figuring, you will only mess things up, and make them worse off than they ever had to be.

Just trust Him in every area of your life, even unto death; He is there with you; blessing you and nurturing you.

The power of God brings about His faithfulness.

His praise is from His temple to the ends of the earth and is fulfilling, God is here, all you need to do is look around you, and you will see Him.

He's right there with you, waiting for you to let Him have His way in your life.

Speaking of the earth that is what you are He made man from the dust of the ground (Adam).

Every time you see the word earth from now on, please be reminded that God is ever present, on the inside of you (Holy Ghost).

That is why you as a Christian should always be in praise and give unto God humble adoration.

This should come easily because of whose you are; praise God from whom all blessings flow, forever and ever, Amen.

A SCATTERED THOUGHT TO PONDER:

What has God done for you?

_____

_____

_____

The Glory of The Lord

(Ezekiel 3:5)

Is In The House!

When you gather in the house of God with other saints, you should always and without any doubt expect to see and feel the glory of God.

God is in the house, and He is desirous of your praise. God has been gracious to you with His Mercy and His Grace. He never forces anyone to do anything, but He certainly wants you too. It should not be hard at all for Christians to give praises to God.

Simply because He is worthy, some men have a big problem giving God praise, but it is time to get beyond that. I know you say it has a lot to do with how you were raised. Well, that is old news, get over it, and get to praising God.

God blesses you each and every day of your life; certainly, the least you can do is raise your hands. That should certainly be enough to get you started; what is so hard about raising your arms in total praise to God?

God, who wakes you up and starts you on your way each and every day,

God who blesses you with good health and gives you strength to do the things you need to do, and want to do, for yourself and your family.

I have observed men many times watching ball games; they give spectacular performances. I watch as they get radically crazy: jumping, slapping hands, and shouting loudly, among other things. It amazes me. Then, they get in church and just sit there and look.

Ask yourself this question, why is that so very easy to do?

And then listen for the response. You are probably not going to like what you hear!

Ezekiel was a man of God with spiritual insight; he saw "the glory of God" returning from the east. He even saw God's glory enter the temple from that same direction. This is an awesome vision that God gave to Him. Imagine the things you would be able to see if you would just praise Him.

Ezekiel was so in-tune to God that the Spirit of God picked him up and placed him in the temple.

Ezekiel watched the glory of God fill the temple; God is still filling His house today.

"I AM" God. Praise me, and honor me, then I will know that you truly love me.

A Scattered thought to ponder:

God is saying to you today, "Men of God, what are you going to do?"

The Requirements of The Lord

(Micah 6:8; 14-15)

Sowing But Not Reaping.

Nothing is more important to God than your personal relationship with Him.

It is His desire that all those that say they are His would get to this place in their life.

Everything that you need to know about God, our Father, is in His Word.

If you don't know it, it could be because you are waiting for someone to spoon-feed you. Every Christian, somewhere along life's way, has to grow up; and get off of the milk of the Word.

There comes a time when you have to encourage yourself and feed yourself from the meat of the Word.

As children of God you have to want to obey, He does not want you to do it because you feel that you should.

He wants you to do it because you love Him and know that you should. In other words, He does not want you to feel burdened by what He is calling you to (obedience).

God requires that we do these things:

Act justly: always be, fair and honest with others. You may be up now, but you have not always been.

Love mercifully: be loyal and always complete your commitment to meet the needs of others. *Walk humbly with God*, don't be arrogant in your fellowship with the Lord always be humble and respectful. When you do justly, you will walk in humbleness, because Mercy covers you, (God's Love).

As in the days of Micah, many were not walking according to the ways of God; it is no coincidence that it is still the same, even today (Micah 2:1-2).

When you are truly committed to the Lord, you will be kind and loving to those around you.

Obey God or pay the penalty because you will certainly and without a doubt reap what you have sown.

In other words, as my sister *Dorris Alexander* would put it; what goes around definitely does come back around (that is the boomerang effect).

You may well be the one to throw it out there, but it is the Word of God that will throw it back to you. God never fails, no never.

A Scattered thought to ponder:

Have you reaped what you've sown?

_____

_____

_____

Satan The Tempter

(James 4:7)

Ways to Resist Him

If you are going to escape the things that your archenemy is sending to you each day it will be through the Word of God.

No man, woman, boy, or girl, has the power to beat Satan alone.

You must solely believe and trust God to bring you through.

Here are positive ways to win out over Satan:

1. You must submit to God; He is your only hope.
2. You must be filled with the Holy Ghost, and led by Him at all times, and you must pray and fast some of the time (St. Luke 4:1-2).
3. You must put on the whole armor of God; this is how you will be able to stand (Ephesians 6:11).
4. You must remain sober at all times (self-controlled) and be vigilant (alert). Satan is walking like a lion, seeking who he can swallow up (spiritually), and it does not matter who you are. His desire is to destroy your testimony for the kingdom of God (1 Peter 5:8), everybody is included in his plan of eternal destruction.
5. Satan will even ask for you; he is a bold spirit. If he asks Jesus for Peter who are we (St. Luke 22:31-32)?
6. You must resist him, and he will flee, (take a stand against him); Satan is not to be played with, you can't win, (James 4:7).

7. You must continue to watch and to pray; these two are connected they go together; if you fail to do this in your life, you will fall to every temptation that comes your way; because your resistance will be low.

The Scriptures define this as, your spirit being willing, but your flesh is weak (St. Matthew 26:41).

These two (flesh and spirit) fight on a daily basis to have complete control over you. Now who do you think is going to win?

Let me help you, if you are doing the things that are mentioned above then the Spirit of God will win you; but if not, then the flesh is certainly the boss; and is ruling, which leaves you open for your enemy to come in, and totally destroy you.

May the Lord God bless you as you search within yourself to make a wise decision because it is a decision that will have an everlasting effect upon you.

A Scattered thought to ponder:

Which direction will you take; will it be the straight and narrow road, which leads to everlasting life, and heaven; or will it be the wide road, which many are already on, that leads to eternal damnation and hell?

God's Victory

(1 Corinthians 10:13)

Is So Real

You can always look to God for victory, and you can even thank Him for the victory you have now; you are not waiting on it to happen, because it has already taken place at the Cross of Calvary.

Jesus Christ died for you and for me then He got up early one Sunday morning, and He declared, that all power was in His hands this is true victory.

Now, this same Jesus is still leading you each and every day, in victory. Won't you thank God? For He has made us a triumphant body of Christians.

We are his instruments, and He uses us as He moves in this world today. The sweet smell is His Word, and it is in every Christian, it is being spread throughout the cities, states, nation, and the entire world (2 Corinthians 2:14).

It is called the Gospel "the Good News" of Jesus Christ; there is no place in this world that it is not.

Victory for the Christian is, that His Word has been hidden in your heart; and that you were the one who did the hiding; and now you are to rejoice, no matter what you may be going through, it will not cause you to sin against the Word of God (Psalm 119:11).

When the Word is deeply rooted inside of you, it leaves no room for you to fail; because you have learned how to walk in the Spirit (Holy Ghost), and you will not desire to do the things of the flesh; bringing them to fulfillment; all of this has been taken away from you by God (Galatians 5:16), you are a new creature, in Christ Jesus.

Victory is also loving God and keeping His commandments; they will not be a burden to you, you will love your brothers and sisters in Christ, in spite of the life that they may be living. You will enjoy doing things in the name of the Lord; you will know that you are His by your new birth, and you will become an over-comer of worldly things, you will have no use for them, because His victory has overcome the world, even – our faith (1 John 5:3-4).

It's all about the Lord Jesus, and the plans that He has for your life; it's not about what you think, or how you may be feeling.

Victory is to know that you are of God; that you are His little children; and that you have overcome them, I ask the Holy Ghost who were them, and I found out that they are the antichrist (false prophet), those who do not believe in God, they are trying with all that is within them to turn you around; but, He goes on to say, greater is He (Holy Ghost) that is in you than he (Satan) that is in this world (1 John 4:4).

This is how you have overcome: with The Holy Ghost, this is true victory in Jesus Christ, Our Lord. Yes, you are free, free from all temptations.

For everyone that comes at you, God has provided you an escape, and He has made you able to bear it all; always look for the way out, that is endurance; not the way in, that is indulgence and failure, before God.

A SCATTERED THOUGHT TO PONDER:

Do you have victory?

Baptism

(St. Mark 10:38-39)

Ambitious Request

Sometimes we ask God for things; but do we really know what we are doing?

You should be very happy that He is God, and that He knows what is best for your life.

He knows exactly what you need and when to give it; He is constantly calling you to Himself and is speaking to you about His love for your life, and also the lives of others.

There are those who go through life looking at others, and desiring what they have; even though you have just what God intends for you to have at this present time.

Why do you want what others have? This is coveting; desiring that of another.

Every Christian is on a different level in their walk with God, but we all need Him.

We have all been at the same level at one time or another in our Christian walk - it was the baptism of the body. Baptism means (1) to be washed, (2) to be buried (to be immersed). The spiritual meaning is this: (3) to pass on sin by the laying on of hands, as ministered in Old Testament days.

What happens in baptism is this, God takes Christ's death, burial, and resurrection; and transposes it to your life. Our old self who is full of sin becomes united with Christ; in His crucifixion and death, and from this baptism, you rise up from the water, into a new life.

This is how you come to obey His holy Word (2 Thessalonians 1:8), and how you dress yourself with Christ Jesus (Galatians 3:26-27).

You do this to show mankind that you have found your new life in Christ, and to show that you are saved from your sins, and even from your own selves.

You should be very grateful that Jesus Christ has done the hard part; that was to die for you. Jesus drank the "Cup" for you and for me; this you should always remember. (St. Mark 14:36) He came not of His own will, but of the will of the Father; therefore, He was obedient and drank the cup of sin.

Now be assured of this, you can never have His glory, and His honor.

No matter what you have done, are doing, or will do, it will never match what Jesus Christ, Our Lord, has done for you.

Jesus did what He did voluntarily; you should follow His example and do the same.

The love that Jesus has for you; and all of mankind, should shine in you so that others may know the real truth, and that they also may be saved from their sins.

Every Christian has a mission in this life; so, find out what yours is, and do it. Jesus Christ came as a Minister, to minister to those who would hear and believe, but; He did not come to be ministered to, (St. Mark 10:45).

Loving Jesus goes past merely saying it; you must also live it, and it should show in your daily walk why? Because somebody truly is watching you!

A SCATTERED THOUGHT TO PONDER:

Does your love for Jesus show? How do you know?

_____

_____

_____

Keep on Going

(1 Kings 18:42-44)

Go Again, And Again, And Again

There are things that you must deal with in your everyday life; things which you do not have the power to do on your own, things that you cannot even see, (spiritual things), but, you still have to deal with them,

That is why you need the Holy Ghost; you need Him to lead you and guide you. Every time you set out to do things on your own, and under your own power, all you do is mess it up.

The Old Testament teaches us how not to give up, no matter what. Elijah had prophesied to King Ahab that there would be no rain for the span of 3 ½ years (1 Kings 17:1).

You must understand that God will use things and circumstances to turn your attention back to Him. You need to be aware of the fact that sometimes there will be droughts in your life, and while you are in your drought you will want it to rain; it will, but it may not come the way that you expect it to.

But don't you give up; just keep on looking, believe, and keep on hoping.

When you are in need of a spiritual breakthrough; pray, and pray with all earnestness, and then God will hear you. After praying, start looking, you may not see anything at first, take a second look, and then a third look, a fourth look, a fifth look, and a sixth look, no matter how long it takes, just keep on looking, keep on praying, and keep on trusting; there will always be one more opportunity, there is a seventh look, and then it shall come to pass.

Elijah sent his servant out seven times (the number seven represents completion and perfection); before He came back and reported that he saw a cloud rising up out of the sea about the size of a man's hand.

It is truly amazing what prayer will do; from the size of the hand of man to covering the whole sky, and then came the rain.

The next verse says that the sky (heavens) became black, the clouds were full of wind; and it began to rain, (heavy). You have to believe that what you have petitioned God for that it will come to pass; no matter how you may be hurting, or how long it may take, wait on Him.

God never fails those that He loves, and He is always there for you, He is an on-time God. The patience comes in knowing that His timing is not ours; so, while you are waiting, use that time to glorify the Father, so continue to stand on the Word of God, and don't you for one second give up on what you believe Him for!

A SCATTERED THOUGHT TO PONDER:

Are you encouraged in your trials?

His Merciful Kindness

(Psalm 117:1-2)

Short But Powerful

Praise is to be performed by everyone, unto the Lord, and by all the nations of this world.

You are to praise God for He is your Creator and Lord; He is to be praised every day and in every way.

When you wake up out of your sleep, the first thing that you should do is; give praise to the Lord God.

You should be giving continuous praises to the Lord, Our God.

Before you lay down to sleep, you should give praises to the Lord, Our God.

You should praise Him, because of His mercy, and His kindness toward you, for it is great.

No one blesses you like "The Lord Jesus Christ," and, low and behold; He is the last one to ever receive the praises of His people.

I praise Him because His truth endures forever and ever; therefore, I will always give praises unto the Lord.

Why do you not praise Him, all of you, people of the earth?

You should praise Him because your destiny (and the destiny of all the people) is involved in what God was doing for His people Israel, and it still is today.

God deserves the highest praise, which is "The Hallelujah Praise," this is the Hallelujah Psalms.

Giving praise to God should not be an afterthought, it should be done just because He is God, and He is worthy (Romans 15:11).

The goodness of God is toward all mankind, and it is left up to you, as to whether you will accept it, or reject it.

But as for me, I have accepted it, and I do it with my whole heart, mind, body, and soul. Yes, He is most definitely, the cause of my praise and the reason for my praise; (Psalm 104:34) and I vow to praise God every day, with a song, and with pleasing meditations. Praise you the Lord, forever and ever, Hallelujah. Amen.

A Scattered thought to ponder:

How often do you praise and thank God?

About the Author

A devoted wife, mother of five, grandmother to ten, and great-grandmother to four, Oregean Adams (lovingly known by most as "Jean"), is known for her wisdom, grace, and love of the Word of God. She is a native of Brinkley, Arkansas, and relocated to the Little Rock area as a teenager.

Jean is loved by many for her honest and genuine personality. She takes pleasure in using her life lessons to be an example and beacon of light for any and everyone she comes in contact with. At the age of 16, she lost her mother. This death was followed by her father at the age of 24 and her daughter at 31. These life tragedies alone are an example of some of the hurdles she has had to endure and overcome early in life and part of her passion for helping others.

She received an online certification from Charles Stanley School of Ministry in the Fall of 2005. In April 2012, she received a certificate of Completion in "Building the Foundation Courses" and "Strengthening the Foundation Ministry Electives" from the St. Luke School of Ministry. Jean is currently an active member of St. Luke Missionary Baptist Church in Jacksonville, Arkansas. Here, under the leadership of Pastor Eric L. Alexander, she has been a member for 20 plus years. She serves as a Minister, Christian Life Development Teacher, and a member of the Prison Ministry, the Prayer Ministry and The Voices of St. Luke.

It is her prayer and desire that the books in her *Scattered Thoughts series* will serve as a resource for Christians to grow in their one-on-one time and that any non-believer who reads it will develop a relationship with Christ.

Word Angels
An Imprint of
Butterfly Typeface Publishing

Iris M. Williams
PO Box 56193
Little Rock AR 72215

(901) 501 - 6653

info@butterflytypeface.com

www.butterflytypeface.com

www.ingramcontent.com/pod-product-compliance
Lightning Source LLC
Chambersburg PA
CBHW081457040426
42446CB00016B/3287